My Blue Goose

Exploiting The Wow Factor In
Real Estate Marketing

For Nicole and Evan

Copyright © Blue Goose Worldwide™ and
Matthew S. Gosselin, 2007 All rights reserved.

This book is printed on acid free paper.

Printed in the United States of America.

LIBRARY OF CONGRESS CATALOGING IN
PUBLICATION DATA
Gosselin, Matthew (Matthew Stephen)
My Blue Goose: Exploiting the Wow Factor
In Real Estate Marketing

ISBN 13: 978-0-615-15941-6
1. Gosselin, Matthew (Matthew Stephen). 2. Real estate business, marketing—United States

Without limiting the rights under copyright reserved above, no part of this publication may be reproduced, stored in or introduced into a retrieval system, or transmitted, in any form or by any means (electronic, mechanical, photocopying, recording or otherwise), without the prior written permission of both the copyright owner and the above publisher of this book.

Susan —
My Favorite Disney
1602 Pal! Can't
Wait To Chat Again!

[signature]

Contents

Forward   **10**

The Story of The Blue Goose   **13**
    Your Blue Goose Is About Being Authentic

Back To The Basics   **21**
    Why Would Anyone Want To Become A Real Estate Professional?
    What People Think of Real Estate Agents
    Finding A Company That Matters
    Some Of The Basics
    What Consumers Want Consumers Get
    Interview With A Top Producer

Contact Construction   **41**
    Building Your Blue List
    The Contacts Are Out There
    Finding Specialized Contacts
    Keep The Conversation Going

Technology and The Internet   **53**
    Even If You Have Wrinkles…
    Watch The Big Dogs and Copy Them
    Websites. If You Build It, Will The come?
    Elements Of A Web Page
    Remarkable Marketing Technology

Advertising Your Blue Goose   **71**
    Elements of Basic Advertising
    Write The Right Way
    Writing To Be Heard

Print Advertising **81**
    Newspaper
    Magazines
    Direct Mail

Internet Marketing **91**
    Facts and Figures
    Forms of Internet Advertising
    Email Marketing

Outdoor Media Advertising **97**
    What is it?
    Pay Attention To The New Trends

Public Relations **101**
    The Basics of PR
    Do Good First
    Interview With A Journalist
    What can I do to get publicity?
    Online Social Networks
    Blogging

Go Guerilla! **113**
    Huh?
    Value of Word of Mouth
    Guerilla Tactics

Wrap-up **121**

Credits **124**

Index **125**

Forward

Forward

I have never been a real estate agent. I've worked in the real estate industry for years but have never had the calling to become an agent. Instead, I have found my niche in learning from and teaching others about good, solid marketing practices that will improve their business. My lessons have come through the study of many companies in and outside the real estate industry. The information in this book does not come overnight. It comes from careful research, thought, and study.

My father once told me, "if you can sell one thing, you can sell anything." It is one of the most valuable sayings I have ever heard. My father also went on to say that if I ever wanted to have complete job security, I should sell toilet paper—a product that no matter how hard times are, people will always need it and buy it. As I would learn, real estate was similar to the toilet paper industry that my dad was talking about. Everyone needs a place to live, right?

I became interested in marketing when I first noticed that companies were selling bottled water. Being from Vermont, I knew that water was fresh and free from just about anywhere so why would anyone want to carry a bottle around with them? According to an article in *Fast Company* in July 2007, bottled water is a $16 billion a year business. Again, why? As I studied this industry at an early age I learned that there wasn't one simple answer. This particular industry was about an evolution.

The professional marketer's key to success is to first understand the formula for what makes products move. How does someone hear about a product? Why are they interested in it? How much do they know about it? How much will they pay? The answers to these seemingly simple questions are what build the foundation for the formula on which we base all marketing whether we are selling toilet paper or homes.

The stories and lessons that follow come from my interaction over the past three years with real estate professionals and I thank each one of them for their insight and honesty so that we all may be better marketing professionals and therefore better real estate professionals.

There are results I cannot claim when you read this book. I can't guarantee that you'll be great in 100 days. I can't guarantee that you will be millionaires within the year. My Blue Goose is about idea generation. You will be able to read through this and say, "yes, I need to apply that to my business," or, "yes, I can do that, but here's how I can do it better." If you are serious about making your business an example that others should follow then this book is certainly for you.

Enjoy the book, but most importantly, enjoy your journey. If I have learned one thing from real estate professionals it is that to be successful one must love what he or she does. It's what makes the bad days go by faster and what keeps the good days plentiful. The real secret is that when you do what you love you also get others excited about it. Passion shines through you. Enjoy and since I don't believe in luck, good skill to you in your real estate career!

The Story of the Blue Goose

"Use What You've Got"
Barbara Corcoran

A few years ago I heard a story that originated in Southwest China about a boy with a blue goose. In America we have a story that is similar in some ways; however, the American tale involves a golden goose.

The story goes that a boy walked his goose 15 miles from his home into town to show it at a gathering of area villages in a local competition. The purpose of the competition was to award the top prize to a goose with the longest bill, because a long bill on a goose was seen as a symbol of power in this culture.

The boy, who I will call "Tom" to Americanize this story, entered the competition and did, in fact, have the goose with the longest bill. But there was also another big difference with this particular goose—it was blue, bluer than the sky. Every other goose in the competition was just white or brown. Although Tom's goose had the longest bill he didn't win the competition because his goose was different from the rest. Tom was desperately disappointed and took his goose back home. He sat with his head in his hands and his parents, trying to be helpful, told him to go with the goose to the wise man of the village. Tom did as he was told and went to visit the wise man. Through tears Tom told the wise man the whole story. The old man sat there with a slight smile on his face. He looked at the boy.

"Young boy," he said, "walk into the village once again with your beautiful blue goose and find the small store at the end of the road. This store does not sell many items because of where it is located, but the owner is humble. Take your blue goose and tell him your story."

The boy, confused, did as he was told once again. He walked back to the village and to the store at the end of the road. Behind the counter was the humble man who listened to Tom's story.

After Tom finished his story, the storeowner said, "I have a great idea. Let's take your beautiful goose and place in my front window so as everyone leaves town they will look at your goose, see its beauty, and its incredibly large bill, which will really brighten their day." The storeowner and the boy made a wonderful nest for the goose. The first person walked past the store and saw the goose. "What a beautiful goose!" the traveler said. "I am about to start a long journey," he told the owner and Tom, "do you mind if I pet your goose as I'm sure it will give me luck for my travels ahead?"

"Sure," the owner said, so the traveler petted the goose. Many others did this as well as they passed by, but it wasn't until that first traveler came back months later with riches found from afar that others realized that the goose was lucky. The blue goose became famous and the storeowner became wealthy because no one else in the village could offer anything so wonderful.

Like most stories this tale has an important lesson. It's even more important because it relates directly to your real estate business—in fact, it relates to any business. Everyone needs some type of blue goose in their business—or, to expose the analogy—an offering that makes you stand out in the crowd. There are more than 1.3 million real estate agents in the United States alone; chances are that you already know many real estate agents; and chances are that you may be related to a real estate agent. In a world of many choices, real estate agents are a dime a dozen. This is probably not the first thing you want to hear, especially if you are new to the real estate biz. What attracts a consumer to a real estate professional is their difference: their difference of service, values, and personality. Defining that blue goose for your real estate business is what this book is all about.

Your Blue Goose is About Being Authentic
Your blue goose is what makes you authentic. Authenticity is what will sell you and your business. It's why brands such as Ben & Jerry's, Starbucks, and Samuel Adams have received their cult-like following. So what does it take to be authentic?

Since you need to stand out in the crowd you need to do things differently. Often real estate professionals are using the same technology; they're working in the same markets; and often they are even using the same branded look. You need to speak louder than your colleagues and since Realtor.com tells us that 40% of real estate agents do not spend a dime on their own marketing, this should not be difficult. Here are a few "must-haves" when discovering your blue goose.

Be Bold
In the past couple of years the market has seen declining sales, declining new construction and there haven't been as many buyers. But it's strange to me. A real estate agent will have a very different conversation with me than they will with a client. With me they will

tell me that business has been slow, sales have declined, and inventory is up higher than it has ever been. Then, they will turn around and tell a client that it is still a great market out there and the media is making it into a bigger deal than it really is. It doesn't take long for consumers to realize that real estate agents are sales people and therefore need to be optimistic about market conditions. The problem is that once they figure this out, they are less likely to turn to that agent for advice. "All of the hard numbers tell me one thing about the market conditions while the agent is painting a whole new picture," said Jack McCarthy, who I met with one afternoon after he and an agent discussed putting his home on the market.

To be bold, agents need to make a stand in situations such as these. Can you imagine a real estate professional writing this message on her marketing materials?

Worst Market Conditions In Eight Years
It's true that we have seen a decline in sales recently, but does that mean we can't sell your home? No, in fact my company has already sold 14 homes in your neighborhood this year. Choosing the RIGHT agent for your home has never been more important.

A message like this delivers the truth, but still packs a payoff punch by letting people know that this agent is a realist, but will still get the job done.

Be Genuine
Originality and authenticity cannot be forced, but it can be promoted. The public relations definition of

doing good and telling people about it applies here. Find something in which you share a passion and tell people about it. Maybe you love animals. On the bottom of all of your marketing you could write that you will share $100 of every sale with the local animal shelter. Maybe you are an avid runner. On all of your materials mention the local upcoming races.

Of course being genuine doesn't end with shared interests. Handwritten notes to people who have taken the time to meet with you are a great way to show you are not only interested, but care to take the time for them.

One agent I interviewed challenged herself to send a gift after every listing appointment she went on. "These people were inviting me into their homes and I realized that for the three years I had been in business I was ignoring a very valuable resource. I decided to make a note of what interests each family had. One woman lived alone and collected the same knick-knacks that my grandmother used to collect. After years of buying them for my grandmother I knew which ones this particular lady was missing and where to find them. She came to my office the same day that she received the gift and we signed papers then and there to list her home. We still talk today, well after the transaction. I also went on a listing appointment and the husband and wife had three boys who all played baseball. I bought them all tickets to a minor league baseball game. The total cost to me was less than $50 and they were very appreciative."

Since this agent has started sending gifts to her clients she has seen her listing presentation successes move from 42% to 85%.

Showing that you have interests outside of selling homes lets people know that you, too, are a real person. Serving a larger purpose is attractive to anyone.

Make Time Your Greatest Gift

Yes, we know, you're a real estate agent and you are very busy. Well, so are your homeowners and there are enough agents out there that they can easily find one that will make the time to help them out.

The first meeting I ever had with a big New York City agent was one in which I walked away in disbelief. He managed to greet me with the nod of his head while talking on the phone and typing an email at the same time. He told me to hold on a minute while he was finishing up. Twenty minutes later I walked out and to this day I'm still not even sure he noticed. He had managed to send three or four emails to people that were clearly not the same people that were on the phone. He was too busy to do one thing at a time. Clearly this is no way to conduct business well.

Integrity Is About Specifics

Very simply put, when you say you are going to do something, do it and do it right. Make sure your marketing really represents you. I have seen many agents advertise a very personable experience, yet they do little more than go through the motions. You have to ask the question if the statement of a personable experience is really specific enough. What exactly does that mean? If you believe this is your blue goose, rethink it. How is your experience personable? What are you doing differently that other agents aren't doing?

"I have integrity," is another statement that doesn't work for the same reason that the vague phrase "personable experience" doesn't work. If you tell a client "I have integrity," their likely first thought is, "Yeah, right; sure you do." Ask yourself "how have I shown integrity in my business?" "What are those specific stories?" "How can I share these stories clearly and creatively in my marketing?"

Begin thinking about the above ideas and how you can make your blue goose take the front window of any store. With these basic values, you will build a solid foundation for your business.

Back To The Basics

*"Nothing is more simple than greatness;
indeed, to be simple is to be great."*
Ralph Waldo Emerson

Why Would Anyone Want to Become a Real Estate Professional?

Not too long ago I was speaking to Elaine, a real estate agent in Pennsylvania who had been in the business for almost 27 years. She was recruited to begin a class to teach the "left-behinds" as the company appropriately calls them. They are the individuals in the upper age bracket that do not embrace technology in their business. Elaine told me about the days in which she first began in real estate.

"I remember carrying large listing books that listed every house for sale in the cities I was working in. It had the owners' name, address, phone number and the real estate agent who was listing the house. To show a buyer a home, I would make all of the appointments a week in advance and confirm them the day before. The problem was that many of my clients did not give me the courtesy of showing up on time for their first appointment and I would have to find a pay phone and call each one of my other clients to let them know we would be late. It was a nightmare."

"It was a different time then," says Phyliss Koch, founder of Koch Real Estate in New York City. "It was nicer. There wasn't the terrible competition that there is now. There were much fewer brokers, and you knew them all. Now you're talking about hundreds and hundreds more brokers, but you're also talking about hundreds and hundreds more apartments."

In my travels I have noticed cut-throat tactics

being used in the bigger cities, such as New York City, Philadelphia, and San Francisco; whereas in rural areas agents seem to be more nonchalant about the business and maybe not quite as aggressive. From the marketing side the agents in the rural areas will most often use customer service and personality as the most prominent selling point and the city-dwelling agents most often use financial acclaims such as "I can get negotiate the best deal for you."

As with any job, real estate is an industry that becomes what you decide to make it. I've seen few agents successful at the part-time agent situation, but it is possible to make a decent income while not turning into one of the 24/7 agents. No matter what environment you work in, know that there is a lot of competition out there.

What Do People Think of Real Estate Agents?

The real estate industry has an uphill battle to change the perception of what the average person thinks of individual real estate agents. If you don't believe me, just Google "Realtors suck" and view any of the 163,000 results that come back. Many of these are blogs and complaints range from agents making too much money when they didn't do much other than list the house on MLS, to one guy that said his real estate agent stole things from his home. One study found that lawyers and car salesman are seen as more trustworthy than real estate agents. A 2006 Harris Interactive poll revealed that 36% of those surveyed felt that real estate professionals had "hardly any prestige at all," indicating that agents have failed to show a lack of real achievement.

There are many bad apples out in the industry and it ruins it for the good agents that are also out there. There are many reasons why this particular industry is littered with sub-par professionals. It could be that to become a real estate agent, you do not need a college education or even a high school education. It could be that the training these days only helps an agent to pass the state licensing test and teaches them very little about how to actually sell a home. It could be that the training is just too short to begin with. Did you know that it would take you longer to train to become a cosmetologist or a nail technologist?

Many who have devoted their lives to the real estate business express their frustration including John Tuccillo, former NAR Chief Economist, who says, "With the expansion of the number of Realtors, the level of competence has fallen to its lowest point ever."

I read an interesting blog from the LakeTahoeRealEstateBlog.com and in it they had a small posting that said, "We tried to sell Crest toothpaste for $35 and didn't get one buyer." They went on to list all of the ways in which they advertised and marketed this toothpaste including direct mail, print ads, sales calls, and so on. Still they did not receive one sale. Their question to the public was, "why?" There are two lessons within this story. The first one is the most obvious. No matter how much you advertise, you will never get anywhere if you don't have the right product at the right price. The second lesson is more important. Real estate agents have all become the Crest toothpaste with a high price tag. The public views agents as though they are all the same and overpriced. Once again, elevating yourself above the others is what you are after—otherwise you wouldn't be reading this book.

Becoming a real estate professional is much more than just receiving your license. It's about the never-ending quest for education to find methods of success to sell a home and to sell yourself.

Finding a Company That Matters
Like most industries, real estate has evolved into consolidated powerhouse corporations, such as Coldwell Banker, Century 21, Prudential, Keller Williams, Sotheby's, RE/MAX, and GMAC. These companies have found that through technology they can consolidate their resources, increase their transactions, and keep overhead costs down. They can do this while promoting a brand of increasing strength. With brand recognition comes the old adage: there is strength in numbers. This is the reason why we are more likely to hear of one of these companies instead of Sally Smith Real Estate who owns just a few offices. These companies are also able to invest large amounts of money into new technology in the hope that with it, they can surge ahead of the competition.

If you haven't already joined a company, ask the important questions, besides what your commission is going to be. Ask what technology makes this company unique. Ask them how they can help you advertise and market yourself. If you really want to be bold, tell them you want to know why you should join their organization over another one that is down the road whose network is just as large. Be sure to ask them what kind of extended training they offer, as every company will offer some sort of new agent training, but few offer solid programs that hire national speakers with the latest and greatest ideas.

Choosing your company is one of the most important decisions you will make. You have already heard stories of certain agents bouncing from one company to another. Remember that by changing companies too often you will greatly increase your chance of losing clients who may be unaware that you have moved.

The truth about becoming a real estate agent is something you won't always hear from those already in the business and especially from the companies who would like to hire you. The reality is that real estate is a very difficult career in the beginning. The reality is that you will spend more hours working in your first six months than you had ever planned. Chances are good that you may not see a check at all for the first six months that you are in business. I would argue that if you aren't able to obtain at least one buyer or seller in a three-month period then this business may not be for you. Simply deciding to become a real estate agent is not enough. Becoming a real estate agent by making smart, well-planned decisions is what will give you success. The ones who tell you they became an agent and were instantly making more money than they ever thought are either being untruthful or are very rare.

It doesn't mean that becoming a real estate professional can't be fun, exciting and rewarding on many levels. I read an article in *Fast Company* that described one real estate broker who told anyone entering the business that "it takes balls to enter into real estate." (Incidentally this is also a quote from the movie *Glengarry Glen Ross*.) This broker was notorious for making a lot of money, but also for losing many agents because of harsh working conditions. I don't agree that real estate has to be that tough. Real estate professionals provide a valuable service. As part of that service, people want to work with an agent with integrity and concern for what they do. That way they know that the agent is genuinely concerned with their business. This fact really does win business.

Interview with a Top Agent

I had the opportunity to sit down with Laurel Strand, a ten-year veteran of the real estate industry in Montclair, California. Laurel has been known as an agent who believes that her business constantly changes, so to keep up with it she has stayed open to new ideas and innovations.

Laurel is a top producer listing and selling approximately 30 homes per year or roughly $20 million in sales each year. I asked her a few pertinent questions.

What has changed most about real estate since you began your career?
"The biggest change has been the introduction of the Internet services and electronic medium of transmitting information about real estate, the market, the realtors and companies. Buyers and sellers are far more knowledge-

able now than they were ten years ago."

Roughly, how much do you spend on your marketing each year?
"I have several marketing systems in place; however, three-quarters are print and one quarter are electronic. All are associated with extremely talented individuals who assist me in executing my business model."

Is there something specific that you have done to drive in the majority of your business?
"Specifically, I created a business model that focused on branding myself and my style within the culture of my neighborhood of Montclair, where I have resided for 25 years."

In your opinion, why do homeowners come back to you for repeat business?
"The public sees me, my product & my success in Montclair. I have developed a reputation for presenting a certain product consistently. The product is a beautiful home. Many neighbors visit my open houses just to say how much they enjoy my presentations. I am highly visible and very accessible to my market."

How many times a year do you contact your sphere of influence?
"Almost weekly, depending on the reason."

How do you contact them?
"Primarily through mailings and casual meetings at their

request for consultations."

In three words or less, give me the secret to real estate success.
"A business model."

Is there anything else you may want to share?
"I think I was lucky to enter [the industry] ten years ago as I had the privilege of working under a number of top-producing agents who are no longer mentoring. I also worked at several companies, learning the importance of branding myself and my style rather than relying on a company to brand me. If I am speaking to a new agent, my best advice would be to follow your instinct rather than prefabricated programs. There are many facets to real estate: commercial, investment, property management—not just residential. I knew that I wanted to be a Montclair specialist from day one.

It just took a few years to develop my business model as I had been told that other agents from other companies dominated Montclair. I had to develop my own identity and a business model based upon my vision & philosophy of selling real estate. The process took about five years. However, I have learned that in residential real estate, solid success rarely happens overnight."

Some of the Basics

Most people forget about the basics of real estate marketing. We get caught up with the newest and most exciting ways of marketing and become distracted and forget about the fundamentals.

There's a chance you also don't remember what the basics of real estate marketing are. We all have stories of sitting through endless days of training, certification, and information overload. Once an agent joins a broker, their new real estate company drags them through more hours of training, speakers, and really bad food. Of course the point in all of this is to teach everyone the basics. However, with so much training, and so much excitement surmounting over your new career, the basics are soon overlooked and then forgotten.

So, first things first. Let's get back to the basics of real estate marketing before we venture into the territory of the "new." Below is a summary of the lessons that you have learned and may have forgotten over the course of your training. Every company out there will tell you that even their basic methods are different; that they are unique and innovative. The truth is that they tell you this to give themselves a more competitive edge and that when you have been to one beginner real estate course, you've been to them all. I can tell you this because I have sat through three of them.

1. Let people know you are in real estate. This sounds so mundane, but telling people that you are in the real estate business is exactly what weeds out the good agents from the bad. Communicating to others on a regular basis will be the defining factor in your career as to whether or not you will be successful. When asked what the number one secret is to becoming a successful real estate agent, Phyllis Pezenik, the sales director for DJK

Residential in New York replied, "It's about constant contact with the buyer and seller." Real estate success could not be summed up any better. Astonishingly, professionals across the United States do not practice this simple rule. Only 16% of real estate agents use direct mail, 15% spend money on advertising on the Internet, and 9% spend money on print advertising. These statistics show us why, "20 percent of real estate agents are making 80 percent of the money according to Jay Costello of Hill & Company in San Francisco.

Think of the people you run into everyday: your bank teller, the person serving at the grocery store, your son/daughter's teachers, neighborhood friends, and everyone at the clubs to which you belong. If you feel weird about telling everyone that you are in real estate, you are probably thinking about those annoying people that you have encountered in your lifetime. The conversations may go something like this:

(At a neighborhood cookout)
SALLY REAL ESTATE: Hi! My name is Sally. I'm a real estate agent.
YOU: Hi Sally, I'...
SALLY REAL ESTATE: Yeah I thought I've seen you before. Hey do you own a home?

This direct approach is not the tack that we want to take. Remember that everything you do reflects on your business and right now the only thing anyone will know about your business is whatever you tell them. The approach just mentioned is too aggressive in all circumstances. Bring up the fact that you are a real estate agent at the right time. Let them ask, "What do you do for a living?" Don't worry, they will ask that question. Tell them, "I'm in real estate. If you know anyone that may need my help, could you give them my name?" This is how you are going to get most of your business, by word of mouth advertising and personal referrals. People love to give recommendations to their friends.

2. Ask People How They Choose a Real Estate Agent. This question will give you an education about how others in the biz get their referrals and in the case of one agent I met, it may even get you a listing. In a casual conversation with her son's teacher, Cheryl learned that the teacher had a negative experience with her agent. Cheryl asked how she found that agent and explained that she was a real estate agent. One thing lead to another and Cheryl was now her son's teacher's new real estate agent. I've heard a hundred stories similar to this one. Again, it was the casual conversation that won the business.

3. Develop a Personal Marketing Budget/Plan. This is the one item in which I see most real estate professionals fail. They forget that this is their business. Every business needs a plan. Imagine wanting to open up a new business and you need a loan. You would walk into the bank and tell them that you would like to start a business. The first question they would ask is, "Have you written a business plan?" Now, business plans can scare most of us—especially if you have no prior business experience.

Writing a marketing plan and budget means sitting down and asking yourself the following questions:

How much do I have to spend on marketing costs without selling a home?
What percentage of my commission will be allocated to marketing costs for the next home?
What times of the year should I market my business?
What are the most cost-effective ways I can get my message out?
What will my company do to help?

The plan itself doesn't need to be as formal as you might think. Writing it will make all the difference in the world.

4. Ask What Your Broker Will Do to Contribute. Your broker and company want you to see those listings just as much as you do. Most companies will help you pay for your marketing. It may help by paying for postcards for you to send out or by paying for an ad in the local paper. Whatever the assistance might be, make sure to take advantage of it.

You should know the right times to ask for more support. For instance, your friend calls you up and tells you that they want you to list their home that is now valued at $950,000. Assuming their price is accurate, walk into your manager's office and explain the situation. Tell them that you believe this listing will require more marketing efforts to sell and is a deserving listing. All offices have money to play with. It will also help you to get your own name out and about and possibly pick up more listings.

5. Price Your Product Right. During a downturn in the market you will hear all of the companies out there stress how important it is to price the house correctly. Why? Because of real estate professionals, like Brian from Maine. Brian is a new agent whom I spoke to at a presentation. At the meeting he told me how excited he was that he had been in the business for three months and he had four listings already. When I checked in with Brian seven months later I was surprised to hear a message that said his office line was disconnected so I contacted the administrator to get his new information. As it turns out, Brian never sold any of the listings that he had. Since he was a new agent with little help from the manager and no mentor, Brian had made a dire mistake. When going to his second listing presentation, he told the homeowner that he believed their house could sell for more. In fact, he thought it would sell for $15,000 more, which was a nice increase since this was only a $215,000 home. In hindsight, the house was really only worth about $205,000 and it was a slowing market. That house stayed listed for the full six month agreement with little to no public interest.

Of course the moral of the story is that getting a listing is a great thing, but if you obtain it with an unreasonable listing price, it will only hurt your business.

6. Everything You Need to Know, You've Learned from Your Parents. It's true: everything your parents told you growing up is applicable to real estate. Here are some quick and fun thoughts to take with you before a listing presentation.

Prior To Your Listing Appointment:
Did you brush your teeth?
Seriously. Did you?

Close the door! You don't live in a barn.
This just reminds me of the time a friend of mine showed up for his very first listing appointment and the cat got out because he had left the door open. To this day the cat has still not been seen (that I know of) and my friend never obtained the listing. True story!

Don't make me get up!
Homeowners can be very kind. They will ask you if you would like something to eat or drink. Unless it is already on the table in front of you, politely decline. Professionalism 101.

You'd forget your head if it wasn't attached to your shoulders!
Make sure you have all of your items before the meeting begins.

You should have that phone surgically implanted in your ear.
Even though this is true for most real estate agents, turn the cell phone off!

About Confidence:
Think before you speak
Even the best listing presenters will practice what they are going to say before they get to their appointment.

<u>Don't break your arm patting yourself on the back.</u>

DO talk about what your company can offer. DON'T brag and tell endless stories about how you are the greatest person on earth. Your personality will sell itself and it does not need explaining.

<u>Enough is Enough!</u>
Don't oversell your services. It will do more damage than good. Being overly boastful is harmful.

<u>If you can Sell One Thing, You Can Sell Anything</u>
A $125,000 listing is just as important as a $1.2 million listing. They both may require different kinds of marketing, but never underestimate a listing. That small listing could lead to many more.

<u>You have an answer for everything, don't you?</u>
It's okay to not know the answer to a question that a homeowner asks. In fact, by telling them you'll have to get back to them with an answer, gives you an excuse to follow up with them again.

The Homeowner:
<u>As long as you live under my roof, you'll do as I say.</u> (What the owner is thinking.) Listen to them like they are giving you the numbers to tonight's lotto.

<u>Don't sit too close to the television, it'll ruin your eyes.</u>
Make sure all of the possible distractions in whatever room you are in are taken care of. This includes your

cell phone!

I don't care what "everyone" is doing; I care what YOU are doing!
It's good to compare yourself to the competition, just don't overdo it.

I will always love you—no matter what.
Although a friend may tell you that, it DOES NOT apply to real estate. This is their biggest investment. Know how to separate friendships and business.

After the listing appointment, do something that most agents say they do, but very few agents truly follow through with it. Follow up your listing appointment with a handwritten thank you note. You are courting these potential clients and you need to make sure you provide an experience that is as personable as possible so they remember you.

7. Know The Basics And Don't Forget Them. Save yourself a lot of money and be careful about investing your money in one of the courses that promises you'll be making millions in x-number of days. There are a lot of them out there. In fact, here is the entire information from just one of the most popular courses: **A.** Make phone calls on a regular basis. **B.** Stop by and physically visit with them on a regular basis. **C.** Write thank you notes all of the time. If you learn these three steps and practice them then you have just saved yourself thousands of dollars. Not to mention these three steps are the absolute bare-bone basics for any salesperson. Not to say that a motivational speech or a good kick in the pants isn't good for everyone every once in a while.

What Consumers Want, Consumers Get

I was giving a presentation in Pennsylvania and I stayed at a wonderful bed and breakfast in a nearby town. The great thing about bed and breakfasts is that people go to them because they want an intimate and personalized experience. At breakfast I was engaged in a conversation with an older couple who was visiting from Florida. They were helping their son find a home as he was planning to move to this town from California. I asked them how their searching was going. Immediately they told me that they were disappointed with the selections that their real estate agent had made. They had multiple conversations and exchanged many emails about the kind of houses they wanted to see. They told the agent over and over that the most important feature they were looking for in a home was a two-car garage. Keep in mind this is a couple that traveled all the way from Florida and their son made the trip from California.

The day they went out house hunting, they looked at ten homes. Guess how many had garages? Zero. When I met with them that morning they had already gone online to a different company and had chosen their new agent.

Your clients and potential clients are more informed than they have ever been. Twenty-four hours a day, seven days a week they have access to more information, studies, and research about the market, the towns and cities, tax laws, and even information about you. So how do you stay ahead of them? Sometimes you can't. Sometimes they will know more about a listing than you do. Why? Because they are talking to their friends about the family that used to live there; they are going to places like Zillow.com to find the past transactions on the house; they are looking up crime rates and educational statistics about the towns. You won't always have this information on the top of your mind, although you should try your best to get as much information as possible. Over 80% of the public researches homes on the Internet before they will talk to you. This fact will not go away.

The most you can be with a client is truthful and real. Concede to the fact if they know more about a property than you do. They still need you to make the transaction happen. You can start the sentence by saying, "Now that I see you're interested in this property, let me find out more information to help you with your decision." This will let them know that you have access to more information, but wanted to wait to understand more of their interests.

Contact Construction
"The easiset kind of relationship is with ten thousand people; the hardest is with one."
Joan Baez. singer/songwriter

Build Your Blue List

Your blue list is your most coveted list. Some companies will call this your sphere of influence (SOI), center of influence (COI) or your farm list. They all mean the same thing. This is a list of at least 100 names and addresses of people that you have contact with on a regular basis. Get their names (remember correct spelling is important!) and addresses and ALWAYS stay in touch with them. Build into your calendar their important dates, like anniversaries and birthdays, so you can send them notes and cards. We'll talk soon about different methods of staying in touch with your blue list, but these are people that you will inform whenever you list or sell a home; when you win an award from your company; when something changes in your own life; and more. It is important to be in touch with your blue list often. They should feel like they are a part of your life and that you know what is happening in theirs. Without this constant contact, and even though you may already have a relationship with these people, they still may not think of you when someone else they know needs a real estate agent.

I was visiting a real estate agent in New York City who told me that they were at their uncle's place for a family Thanksgiving dinner. Over the course of dinner, their Uncle asked how this agent's job was going. The agent told him that she just received her third listing that month and that she was pleased with her business. Her uncle's response upset her. He told her that he forgot she gave up her last job to become a real estate agent and said, "I wish I'd remembered because our neighbors just asked me if I knew anyone in real estate. They were in the market and looking for an agent." He'd told them he couldn't think of anyone. The real problem here was that it was a $3.6 million listing. They'd signed with an agent the day before this Thanksgiving dinner.

This situation is much more common than you think and it will happen to you unless you do a good job of staying in touch with everyone you know. If you are comfortable with it, stay personal with this list. Let them know, for instance, that you and your husband just had a healthy baby boy and tell them "as my family grows and as your needs change, I am here for all of your real estate needs. Find every excuse to stay in touch with your blue list like a teenager waiting to call the boy of her dreams.

The Contacts Are Out There

You may be wondering, "What if I can't find 100–200 names to work with?" Don't fret—there are a number of ways to receive names of consumers who may be interested in your real estate services. It's important to note that nationally, 14% of homeowners move every year, according to the Mayflower Transit Company. This fact stresses the importance of creating a list of at LEAST 100 names so that you will always be sending information to more than seven people who are in the market for real estate services. Below are just a few techniques you can use to obtain more solid leads.

1. Fishbowl. Place glass jars (or fishbowls) at various restaurant counters around town. Naturally you'll have to get the permission of the owner before doing this. The reason the restaurant owner will allow you to do this is because you will be offering any homeowner who drops their business card or name/address into the bowl, a chance to win a $50 gift card to that particular restaurant.

On a sign above the glass jar write:

Dear Homeowner,

Enter your business card or name and address here for a chance to win a $50 gift card to this restaurant.

I'll also be sure not to call you, but to mail housing market statistics to you about the area in which you live!

Sincerely,
Jane Real Estate

What you've done here is to offer patrons of the restaurant a chance to eat at their favorite place for free. Everyone knows that when they drop their name and address in a jar they are going to be called or someone is going to try to sell them something. For this reason, let them know that you will be mailing them some market information that they will want anyway. Everyone is always curious about how much their neighbor's homes are worth.

2. Quarterly Calls. I spoke at one real estate company who had set up an event for their agents called "Thursday Night Contacts." Once a quarter the company would open up a couple of their offices and buy pizza, beer, and soda for the agents to give them a scheduled call to call their blue list group. I'll be the first to tell you that I do not like telemarketing. Rest assured that this is much different. This is not cold-calling people that you have never spoken to before. These are your aunts, uncles, close friends, people you attend church with, neighbors, and so on.

This company recognized that their agents were so busy during the day setting up appointments that they rarely had time to contact the people most important to their business. Within the first two quarters that the company began Thursday Night Contacts, they saw listings grow 18% at a time when their competitors saw decreased listings on market.

The agents began getting very creative as well. Here are some of the comments I heard:

"Each time I called someone, I very briefly made notes of what we talked about in my Excel sheet. For instance, Jan told me that her daughter was graduating from high school in a couple of months. I made a note of that and when I called her back the next quarter, she was very impressed when I asked her about how far along her daughter was in getting ready for college in the fall."

"I arm myself with statistics that I pull from our company resources and after we talk about the weather, the kids, or whatever, I mention that the reason I was calling is that I wanted to let them know that the value on their home has risen an estimated 5% in the past year. Thanks to computers, I can look up this information while I am on the phone with them. They think I am looking out for them, so why would they ever choose another real estate professional?"

"I've been in real estate for over 20 years and everyone knows what I do. There is no need for me to read them a script about how important it is to list your home at the right time. So, most of my calls are of a personal nature 98% of the time." The long-term relationships are the advantage that many of the experienced agents have, but they still require regular maintenance.

3. Clubs and Events. There is a real estate professional in Rhode Island who I must keep nameless. Ten years ago, and to the dismay of his wife, he decided to join a brand new private golf club. He justified it by telling his wife that he could take clients there and maybe even pick up a few of the members as clients.

Over the course of the first year he introduced himself to absolutely anyone he saw and asked them if they would want to play a round together sometime. Most often they said yes. As members they knew it was important to get to know the others involved in the club.

"It helped that he wasn't overly aggressive or annoying," the pro shop manager told me. "In the first two years, I never saw him playing with the same three people."

What makes this work is that anyone who joins the club as a new member also receives a brochure in their folder from this real estate professional that is titled: *I sold 43 member homes last year and I'll sell yours too!*

To this day, this real estate professional does not set foot in his office. He has a closing team that will show homes to his clients and conduct all of the paperwork for him. He provides his team a nice bonus at the end of the year. Everyone at this golf club knows that if they have any real estate questions they have their own personal real estate consultant at their golf club.

I'm not telling you to purchase a golf club membership. The point is that we are all involved with charity groups, social clubs, and church groups and have intimate access to a group in which we share common interests. People are thankful when they have someone they can turn to and who they know will do what is best for them and their real estate investment. To ignore marketing within these different groups is a big loss.

4. Rescue a "For Sale By Owner" (FSBO) This group is often neglected because they are viewed as a threat to real estate professionals. In fact, very often agents and FSBOs are an "us against them" scenario and it shouldn't be that way. In an editorial column in the Orlando Sentinel, one homeowner said, "I'm ticked off at Realtors. I ask you why you don't show my house that is for sale by owner and tell you that I am paying a 3% commission and you tell me that is not enough. Since when is more than $9,000 not enough? Wake up you prima donnas. You aren't surgeons."

The tensions between agents and FSBOs don't warrant that the two should leave each alone. According to the National Association of Realtors, residential real estate transactions conducted by homeowners accounted for 9% of the total market in 2003. The number of those *attempting* to sell without the use of a real estate agent is much higher.

Real estate has quickly become a technology-driven business and many of these technologies are not yet easily available to non-professionals. For this reason, along with inaccurate pricing, understanding the paperwork and getting the home ready for sale, owners get frustrated and will fire themselves. This leaves an excellent opportunity for an agent to rescue the homeowner.

The rescue does not begin at the failure of the homeowner. Instead, seek out for sale by owner homes and introduce yourself whether it is a personalized email, phone call or face-to-face meeting. Offer them advice and to answer any questions they may have to help them sell your home. The fact remains that most people do not want to go through the work of listing their own home and it may turn into a client for you and certainly another name for your blue list.

5. Invest In A Business Card Reader. All of the above ideas would be better aided with a business card reader. These readers allow you to run many business cards through the machine all at once and it will compile the information for you into a spreadsheet. Do yourself a favor and search for one on Froogle or Amazon. It will save you a lot of time so you won't be stuck punching keys all week.

6. Property Business Cards. This new and inexpensive marketing piece has been a hit with real estate agents on the West Coast. With each listing, agents will place a photo or two of the listing, the price, and the MLS number and when you flip the card over, it is the agent's typical business card information. What makes this work so well is that the agents will give this card to the homeowners who then pass them around within their network. The homeowner passes the card out because they want to show off and sell their house more than you do. What they are also doing is referring your services to the friends and family. In the marketing world this is called a silent referral, but it is also seen as a form of guerilla marketing. We'll talk about guerilla marketing soon.

Finding Specialized Contact Lists

There are times when you will need a contact list that is very detailed and your blue list will not satisfy what you need to be successful at marketing a particular property. One of these times will be when you are working with a developer and need to sell several units to a specific group of people. One example that comes to mind is a community up in the Lakes Region of New Hampshire. An agent was working with a developer on a community that had its own landing strip and homes that started at $1.5 million. These types of properties are only being sought out by a select group of people.

This developer and the agent worked together to come up with plan that involved getting names and addresses of any executive in the Northeast that flew or owned their own plane.

These types of lists can be purchased from one of many companies out there, such as infousa.com, Equifax, Experian, or Transunion. Of course, these companies charge a fee for the lists and the more detailed list you need, the more expensive the price tag.

Before you purchase these lists, contact your company's marketing department to find out if they have already bought a similar list, or if they have a subscription to a company that would allow them to pull the list for free.

Keeping The Conversation Going

I've heard over and over again from many agents that they are not sure why they should contact their blue list. They fear they don't have a good enough reason to. I'm here to tell you that any reason is a good enough reason to stay in touch with the list that is going to bring you the most loyal business. Rarely have I ever worried that a real estate professional is contacting their list too often. Any solid business relationship is about having a conversation. It's a conversation through many forms of contact.

Below are just some of the excuses, holidays, and events for calling, mailing, emailing, or talking to the clients on your blue list.

New Year's Day
Martin Luther King, Jr. Day,
Chinese/Lunar New Year
Lincoln's Birthday
Valentine's Day
President's Day, U.S
Family Day, Canada
Ash Wednesday
Orthodox Lent Begins
Washington's Birthday
St. Patrick's Day
Spring Equinox
Palm Sunday
Daylight Saving Time Begins
Jewish Passover
Easter Sunday
Orthodox Easter Sunday
Cinco de Mayo

Mother's Day
Memorial Day
Father's Day
Summer Solstice
Independence Day
Labor Day
Grandparent's Day
Fall Equinox
Jewish New Year
Yom Kippur
Columbus Day
Daylight Saving Time Ends
Halloween
Election Day, U.S.
Veteran's Day
Thanksgiving Day
Winter Solstice
Christmas Day
New Year's Eve
Graduations
Sporting Event Celebrations
College/High School Homecomings

The great thing about having the list above is that it reaffirms that you should be speaking with your blue list all of the time. Statistically and for the greatest success you should contact your blue list a minimum of six times a year. Doing so puts you in front of the right crowd at the right time so when they are in the housing market, they have no reason not to consider you.

The Internet and Technology
"Technology has advanced more in the last thirty years than in the previous two thousand. The exponential increase in advancement will only continue."
Neils Bohr, Danish Physicist (1885–1962)

Even If You Have Wrinkles, Embrace It!

I want to preface this section with the bold statement that if you are one of those agents who would rather not deal with technology and are not interested in trying, this is not the business for you. Technology has and will continue to change the way the real estate business is conducted. If the kitchen is too hot for you, you ought not become a chef, as the saying goes.

Earlier I wrote about Elaine, an agent who was asked by her company to teach the "Left Behinds"—a group of like-minded individuals who haven't yet embraced technology.

Elaine spent a couple of years taking courses, buying a computer for her house and learning everything she could about technology. She now tells everyone, "I was hopeless with computers; I didn't like them because they scared me, but when it came down to it, learning how to use them was easy. If I can do it, then you can."

Due to the Left Behind's longevity in the real estate business, many of these agents feel no need to change their business model because, as one agent put it, "These people have known me for years and they won't go to someone else." Unfortunately, if you are an agent who shares this opinion, you are in for a rude awakening. Many of the Left Behinds are losing business to better technologically-aware competitors, because they can respond fast; they are able to retrieve information faster; and can close deals more effectively and efficiently than those who do not embrace technology.

One example is 30-year resident, Raymond O'Toole, of Braintree, Massachusetts. Raymond, an owner of several properties in the area, has used the same real estate agent in 14 of his last 15 sales. For his last listing he did not use the agent that he had used for so many years. Why? As he puts it, he needed to move fast on the sale of this particular town home and knew that his usual agent did not have the technology to meet his needs.

"Gerry and I had a business relationship for more than 23 years. We often joked about how technology was going to be the doom of good personable business relationships. I believed that up until a couple of years ago. Unfortunately Gerry still believes that to be true, which is why he does not check and respond to emails even though his company has provided him with the tools he needs. When he gets an email, he responds by calling the person directly even if it is for a quick answer. When I email someone with a quick question I expect a quick email back. I don't have time to continually answer the phone," said Raymond.

"There were many other things that Gerry could not offer me that others did. For instance, with most agents now, I can get pictures taken and placed on a website in the same day I list the home. Gerry still doesn't own a digital camera. "When it came down to it, I knew it was time for a change. I still have lunch with Gerry every now and then and we continue to be friends, but he still thinks that using technology leads to bad business."

Don't be afraid of technology. Everyone is afraid of making mistakes. Everyone is afraid of looking stupid. I don't have a problem with it. I look stupid on most days of my life. The best of us have a fear of looking dumb and when we don't try something we don't know or understand it we avoid it. Here's your last warning for all of those still not making the effort to learn these new technologies: GET WITH IT!

Watch the Big Dogs and Copy Them

If the Coca-Cola's and Disneys of the world used the approach that some of the agents are using today, long ago we would have been raving about Pepsi and Universal Studios. There is no reason why a one-person business can't look at their business the same way a Fortune 500 company does. As a case in point, let's look at a few and how they maintain personal relationships while using the Internet to better their business.

Papa John's Pizza: As small as it was, Papa John's was one of the first pizza companies to truly embrace the idea of ordering pizzas online. As a result, they have captured the college markets in their areas. Their grasp of technology continues within their management and infrastructure giving them an efficiency over competitors.

"Papa John's Information Systems (I.S.) department offers a wealth of technological resources to our franchise family. We employ the same in-store technology, the Papa John's PROFIT System™, system-wide, providing a solid, state-of-the-art system platform for pizza restaurant management. The I.S. team installs and provides training on the Papa John's PROFIT System™ in each restaurant and also offers ongoing support through the Papa John's Help Desk.

The Corcoran Group: The Corcoran Group was one of the first real estate companies to use video as a way to showcase new listings to potential buyers. In Barbara Cororan's book *Use What You've Got (Portfolio, February, 2003)*, she explains that the initial idea was to video tape each home and play it on a TV that would be street-facing. Of course this idea later evolved into the virtual tours and other home video tours that can be found just about anywhere. The benefit of using video is obvious. Homebuyers can tour a home without ever leaving their computer. Cutting edge companies like The Corcoran Group will continue to pave the road for best real estate practices.

Expedia.com: Expedia.com began in 1995 and is now the 4th largest travel agency in the world. It didn't happen overnight, but it was close to it. Founders, Richard Barton and Lloyd Frink knew that there was a need in the travel world and it needed to be met. Travelers were spending too much of their time on the phone with travel agents, and the agents would be bogged down by all of the changes to just one itinerary—a very time consuming process. Expedia used the immediacy of the Internet to provide fast quotes on vacations along with comparisons and general travel information. The move changed the industry and made all of us more efficient.

Although Expedia is in the travel industry, their idea of efficiency using technology can be incorporated into real estate.

Websites: If You Build It Will They Come?

I have seen some great websites in the real estate world. I have also seen some websites that are a waste of someone's money. Websites are a part of a brand identity—the personality of company or of a person. I tell new real estate professionals that the first thing they need to look at is the company's website and how much money the company is willing to invest into it. This is important because more than 85% of home searches begin on the Internet (NAR). Everyone knows that real estate is a race: a race to be the first seen by the consumer. The first to be seen is the most likely one to close the deal.

Still the question that remains to be answered is, if you are part of a company with a great website, is it necessary that you have one as well?

To answer this question we need to look outside the real estate industry. There is a new business tool that many Fortune 500 companies are using today. They are called microsites. Microsites are a supplement to a company's main site. Most often these sites use catchy phrases like a mattress company's www.GiveMeSomeRest.com, or Tabasco sauce's once-used www.ILikeItHot.com. Their main purpose is to attract attention to a specific product or service and to allow that interest to be measured accurately. These sites will often provide more intimate and casual information about the company or service.

Real Estate professionals should follow a similar practice. The Coldwell Banker's, Prudential's, Century 21's and GMAC's of the world spend millions of dollars a year on developing and maintaining their websites and it is a waste of an agent's dollar to attempt to recreate sites like these. That doesn't mean that an agent should not have a presence on the web, which is where these microsites come into play. The microsites provide content that their company can't or won't provide.

Elements of a Great Website
When building your site, ask yourself questions like, what is the most important thing that a person looking at my website will want to know? Why would anyone want to visit my site? Do they understand the value they can get from my site within the first 30 seconds of being there? Here are some must-haves when designing your site.

Everyone Loves a Story: Detailed information about your experience with the town will interest your Internet readers. After all, they are on your page to learn more about you. How well you know the school system, your knowledge of events, and your favorite thing about the town are all points to include. Don't make it into a book, but be thorough.

Who's in Charge? Write out a list of all of the town officials and/or mayor with email addresses if possible. This will act as an important resource should anyone want to ask questions about building/renovation permits or general questions about the city or town. Often cities and towns don't have the greatest websites and this information can be difficult to find.

Where Do I Go? It's important to put yourself in the buyer's shoes. What questions would they ask? They may want your take on the best places to eat, shop, and to be entertained. Provide short descriptions about your personal preferences, because you aren't just selling a house, you are selling a lifestyle.

What's In a Name? Now, ideally the name of your dot com can be your personal name i.e. JanRealtor.com or it can be something more creative like IKnowEverythingAbout(YourTown).com. If you are able to, try to abbreviate your name so your address will be as short as possible. This will make things easier for your marketing efforts and the ability of people to remember your address.

Clutter Is Chaos: The organization of your website is just as important as the content in it. Companies throughout the world spend millions of dollars hiring user interface professionals to make sure that their readers are not overwhelmed with the content on the website.

Blog It: What can you offer that no one else in the world can? Your opinion. Give your readers a reason to come back to your page by keeping your blog neat and up to date on your website. To position yourself as a real estate resource, interpret sales reports for your readers, create interesting headlines, and offer advice. Once you have blogged for about a year there will be very few people who can or will even try to offer as much information as you have given about the local real estate market.

If you make a prediction and it comes true, share that with your readers. Title it "Flashback: Jane Agent predicted an increase in home sales in May of 2006." These kinds of tactics give further credibility to your site and to you. More importantly, with a simple press release you may find yourself in the local paper.

Create A Concierge Page: As every agent needs to distinguish themselves from the competition, developing a concierge page that helps promote your blue goose features.
You deserve first class service. Here are just some of the things I do for each one of my listings:
Professional photography
Dedicated web page with unique web address (i.e. www.123mainstreet.com
Home cleaning services the day before open house
Dog walking service during open houses
Fresh flowers brought in for each open house
Property business cards so you can promote your property to your friends and family
Free magazine forwarding service
Free custom direct mail Just Moved postcards

Setting yourself apart from the other agents is easier than you think. Give people a reason to be excited about doing business with you. Remember that they are attracted to authenticity and you've got it!

Remarkable Marketing Technology

Someone once asked me, "Matt, what is the one most important element of real estate?" to which I replied, "Technology." Their next question was simply, "Why?" It's absolutely true that technology is changing the way we do business. It has changed the way the world conducts its business. By the time you read what I believe are the latest and most exciting technology advancements relating to real estate, they will likely all be old news. It doesn't make the following companies any less important though. These companies will continue to lead the way within their respective interests and other companies will be created to help real estate selling become more efficient, less expensive, and to achieve a level of customization that has never been done before. Without the use of this new technology, real estate professionals will fall behind the pack, creating new opportunities for those who embrace it.

The descriptions of some of the best new technologies are listed below, but keep in mind that they are simple summaries of what these services offer. As great as these companies and their services are, they will not do anything for you if you don't check them out yourself. When developing your annual marketing plan it is important to look at all that is available to you each year and plan accordingly. This, of course, will help you to stay within your budget and overall business plan.

LeadRouter: This is a lead management tool that gives its users a "wow" factor in response time. Users of this tool claim that although there is a slight learning curve with programming the software, the results are outstanding.

The idea is simple. Consumers visit a real estate website and when they click a button to request more information about a property or service, a text message with appropriate contact information is immediately sent to an agent's cell phone. It is at that point that an agent can respond immediately or pass the potential lead to the next agent in line.

The NRT company (now under Apollo) has since purchased this technology outright to make it exclusive to Century 21, ERA, Sothebys, and Coldwell Banker.

SpotRunner (www.spotrunner.com): This is a special tool that has been created for many industries, not just real estate. As with most new technology, it has created a solution for what used to be a time-consuming and very expensive problem. Ask yourself this question, "How many commercials have I seen on the television, which advertise just one agent?" We're not talking about commercials that advertise a large company; we are talking about Jane Realtor having her own commercial. This site makes it possible.

The registration is very easy. Signing up for a Yahoo email account is much more difficult. Once you have registered, you can browse through a selection of pre-made professional commercials, which will allow you to upload your own photos, logos, and company information. The cost to buying one of these commercials starts at around $499 as of 2007. Once your commercial is selected and you have customized it, you are then able to pick the stations and times in which you would like your commercial to air. This process alone can save a significant bundle of money because it takes away a media buyer who often will mark up these spots by 15% for their commission. The downside is that when dealing with large budgets, media buyers can also negotiate lower rates. You are not able to negotiate on SpotRunner. However, the reality is that you probably do not have a large budget to work with anyway, which makes this irrelevant.

After you have completed filling in your information, SpotRunner will send you your commercial with your information, photos, and logos and will air it for you. Don't believe it? Watch any station during the times that you requested and it will air.

Xpressdocs (www.xpressdocs.com): This is said to be the leading on-demand printer for the real estate industry. It prides itself as being a technology company first and a printer second. By creating a business model around technology it gives the company the opportunity to create programming tailored to the companies that use it, so it is not a "what you see is what you get" situation.

Established in 1998 by an airline pilot, Xpressdocs quickly found a way to allow real estate agents to order products by 5 p.m. EST, and receive them the next afternoon. The user can login, choose templates that most often are designed by their own company, personalize the templates, and even add in their own photos and text. From there the user will decide to have all of the products sent directly to themselves or in the case of postcards and brochures, have Xpressdocs mail them out immediately to the agent's own mailing list or a list that Xpressdocs provides. Postcards, brochures (tri-folds as well), flyers, business cards can all be ordered from this system. The quality is the highest that I have seen, complete with UV coating and are printed on the high quality paper.

VHT: There are many companies out there that offer professional photography, 360-degree tours, and floor plan creation, but in my opinion there are few companies that embrace technology as well as VHT. They have effortlessly managed to deliver options to agents, such as including photos onto cable television services and automated photo delivery onto print marketing websites. What makes this company so exciting is their commitment in creating the most cutting edge technologies while listening to real estate professionals' needs. It allows for companies to integrate the VHT systems into their existing intranets.

With over 150 professional photographers, VHT serves more than 55,000 clients and have photographed over $1 billion in residential real estate alone.

FloorPlanOnline.com: As a relatively new company, FloorPlanOnline offers a unique service that greatly distinguishes it from the many virtual tour companies. Floorplan Online combines the visual of a home's floor plan with actual photos taken of that home. It allows the users to click on camera icons and view the home from that particular area and unlike a virtual tour, the user knows precisely where the room is located within the home.

The simplicity in this system is what makes the site so exciting. Additionally, it gives agents the ability to assign a specific domain name (123MainStreet.com) to the floor plan making accessibility for potential buyers memorable and easy.

Zillow: I will not be the first to tell you that in general zillow.com is not a favorite among real estate professionals. I will argue that agents need to become familiar with this technology simply because Zillow is a friend of your potential clients.

Zillow provides tools to the public to help them learn the value of their home, list their home and find other homes in their market and beyond. What has made Zillow so controversial is their Zestimate, a tool that uses information from tax records to estimate the value of a home. The Zestimates are not always accurate, but are improving every day.

More and more features are being added all the time, like one of my favorites that mocks the day when someone would leave a note at the door that offered a certain amount of money for their home whether the owners were selling it or not. Zillow calls it "Make Me Move™."

The name of Zillow is said to come from the idea that zillions of data points would have to be found to create the network, but these data points represent more than just plain old data points. They represent homes—a place where people rest on their pillows. So using zillions and pillow, the name Zillow was formed.

As professionals in the industry you need to

understand the technologies that your consumers are using. Zillow is no exception. The smart ones will figure out how to make Zillow part of their blue goose by incorporating the technology into their own website.

Craigslist: Craigslist has taken over where national newspapers have lacked. It is a no-frills site that is simply an online classified page. The site is known for the loyalty of its users. It has long been the #1 classified site on the web.

The real estate side began with many listings coming from owners. It wasn't long before large companies joined in and produced tools for their agents to use in conjunction with Craigslist. Since it is currently free to list homes, many agents have jumped on board and listed most all of their homes on the site.

Craigslist, at some point, may charge fees for many of its services. However, these fees will remain low and agents will continue to use it despite the costs. Jumping on board early will give you even more leverage in the marketplace.

Try to do more than simply place a listing on the site. You are able to use templates that will give your listing an attractive look. One company is www.classified-flyerads.com. Choose your color, layout, and how many photos you would like and it will do the rest for you.

MySpace: There are many people who believe that sites such as MySpace, Facebook, and Linkedin have no place in the real estate business. I am a big believer in the creed of "in your face every place..." especially when it's free. Will you see much of a response from any of these websites?—probably not, but it does give you one more place where people are likely to make contact with you and it requires very little maintenance.

You can design your own page and create your own community and friends very easily. I would encourage you to post blogs that you have written about local and national real estate conditions. Also use it for major personal updates. People love to feel like they know what is going on with your life. You'll also be surprised with the number of people that are on the site with whom you may have lost contact over the years, especially if they are in your community. You may be able to pick up listings.

Second Life: As at the publishing of this book, Second Life is just now making waves in the business world. In fact, let's not call them waves, but small ripples instead. View Second Life as a chat room where you can now view each person with whom you are talking. You are really viewing their Avatar, a character they custom create and clothe. What makes Second Life so interesting are not necessarily what the site is now, but what it will become. Currently companies can buy islands in this virtual land. The real estate implications for Second Life are endless. For now, most people could use it as a resource tool. Buy your own island for United States real estate advice (remember this site is international). You can become an area where homeowners can ask you relevant real estate questions. It won't be long until you will be able to show listings in this world—maybe even island listings! Coldwell Banker was the first known large real estate company to buy their own island. If it's good enough for them, it's good enough for your business too.

    I strongly urge you to take a look at this new virtual world because in five years it will certainly become part of yours.

Advertising Your Blue Goose

"Never write an advertisement which you wouldn't want your family to read. You wouldn't tell lies to your own wife; don't tell them to mine."
~David Ogilvy

Elements of Basic Advertising

Whether you have hired someone to create an advertisement for your business or are doing it yourself, there are some basic elements to an ad that you must include.

Your name.

Your contact information, which includes at least one phone number and an email address.

A website address.

A photo. Do not create an ad that is all text. Incorporate a photo whether it is of you, a home, or another relevant image.

Equal housing logo and legal disclaimer. You can find this information on www.hud.gov

Write the Right Way

Every agent needs to understand why it's not always a great thing to be cute with advertising and why taking the higher road of professionalism will most often win out. Understanding how to write creatively, clearly, and correctly are all important parts of the advertising process. All of these skills help your business to look as though you have hired a professional marketer to create your materials. This adds credibility to your business.

In my travels throughout the country I have heard so many agents tell me that they can't write well. It seems that people are most afraid of sounding dumb when they write so they don't even try. What is a good writer? Writing well is simply communicating your message so your audience understands it. That's it! Getting them to want to read it is more about writing creatively, not writing well. Don't worry about that just yet, we'll get into it.

I've compiled a short list of refreshers for you. I don't care even if you are an English teacher—it is always good to read these from time to time. I once had a tough professor who used to ask me, "If I allow you to make mistakes on your papers, how many mistakes will you allow me to make when I write your recommendation letter?" I got the point right away and told him that he could make no mistakes on it since I wanted him to sound credible. His reply to that was, "Okay then, for every mistake you make on a paper, I'm taking 10 points off." If I made more than four mistakes on a seven-page paper for instance, I failed. If that's not motivation, I don't know what is. Be thankful I'm not going to test you on these following tips!

Speak Out Loud What You Are Writing: If it doesn't make sense when you are saying it, then it certainly won't make sense to the person reading it.

God Made Punctuation—Use It: From the early days of our schooling we have been afraid of using punctuation. But using punctuation will help the reader understand your conversation style and allows you to emphasize certain words to get your point across. Now that you will be using punctuation again after so many years, be sure you don't over-punctuate.

The great thing about using punctuation is that since you will be using this mostly for your advertising, it is difficult to mess up. Often advertisers do not use punctuation that will impress your high school English teacher, but instead they use it to make certain words and sentences stand out. Here is a quick punctuation review for you:

Periods: You'd be surprised how many people for get to place a period after a sentence to let the reader know to pause. Remember that if you are bulleting information, you do not need a period. Bullets are usually not complete sentences.

Commas: When you're writing down a thought and you want to take a breath, whether mental or physical, place a comma.

Exclamation Point: Use this when you're really excited about something. You almost never need to use more than one in a paragraph.

Colon: Use this when you want to make an example of something: For example, just like this.

Semi-colon: Put these in your writing in the place where, in conversation, you'd arch your eyebrow or make some other sort of physical gesture, signaling that you want to emphasize a point.

Question Mark: Obviously, when you have written a question.

Dashes: You can use these when you've already used a colon or a semi-colon in a sentence, but be aware that if you have more than one colon or semi-colon in a sentence, you're probably doing something wrong.

Shorter Is Better: The average consumer will pickup a postcard and read it for about 4.5 seconds. They may look at your ad in a newspaper for about the same amount of time. Before you write your message define three points that you want your reader to take away. For

example:
> I have lived in this community for 30 years.
>
> I have sold over 30 homes. (Notice I said *over* 30 homes instead of 31. It makes any number sound larger.)
>
> Visit my website.

Now that we have our three points we need to find a way to piece them together to sound conversational:

"As a 30-year resident of Burlington I know how important it is to find the right home. Last year I gave over 30 homeowners keys to their new homes and I want to do the same for you. Visit my website at www.your-website.com."

With just a few sentences you have given your experience, your success and a place where they can read more about you on their own time.

Use Words You Know And Are Real: Do not use slang. I've seen too many bad outcomes. Remember that you need to sound as professional as you can without sounding like a textbook. When you are writing to your community you should be using your own voice as if you were speaking to them in person. For that reason, don't pull out a thesaurus and try to use words you have never used before.

Grammar Does Matter But Not As Much As You Think: The one good thing you have going for you in the grammar arena is that chances are you have been educated well enough to know the basics. Be confident that the basics are enough.

Try To Write Well Every Single Time You Write: I have read a lot in my lifetime: magazines, books, advertising copy, scripts—you get the idea. There is one secret I have learned that seems to remain true. When a person sits down, thinks about what to write with no distractions, and takes the time to review their work, they are very often considered good writers. It makes sense. Why else do you hear of famous authors secluding themselves from the rest of society to write their best-selling novel? Stephen King lives in Bangor, Maine. Do you think he has a lot of distractions up that way? Don't think you are any different than these people. Yes, it's true you are not writing the great American novel, but nevertheless, by taking the time to write and review what you are writing, chances are you will be considered a good writer.

Read it backwards: When proofreading, read it backwards. It will help you to pick up the spelling errors by forcing you to look at each and every word.

Writing To Be Heard

Let me preface this section about copywriting by telling you to remember that everyone is born creative; everyone is given a box of crayons in kindergarten.

Find Your Voice: I have a mentor who is an author. He used to tell me all of the time "Matt, you need to find your voice." His suggestion really ticked me off. It took me four years to find my voice because he would never tell me more than that. It didn't matter how hard I pressed or even insulted him, he wouldn't give me more information. I am going to save you four years of your life and tell you that finding your voice simply means that you first need to learn how to tell an interesting story. Then, you write it down using the same language that you would use if you were talking to your best friend. Creative writing is all about finding that charming talk that you use in casual conversation.

So, what makes an advertisement creative? Creative advertising can be defined as catching someone off guard or saying something that isn't heard too often. If you are the average agent out there I can just about tell you exactly what you are going to write on a postcard before you write it. Why? If I pick up a postcard that a real estate professional has sent to me, it is going to tell me that this real estate guru wants my business. In fact, that's exactly the point we all want to get across. Let's be clever about it though.

I am so tired of the cheesy advertising out in the real estate world and quite frankly, the public does not care to see it either. "I'm your secret agent," one agent claims sporting an oversized trench coat that makes him look like one of those flasher dolls you see at the joke store. "Let me be your Home-ee." What is this person trying to say? "My name is Joe Block. I'll sell your whole block." Are you kidding me? This is not the kind of advertising we are trying to send out.

Here are some ideas to get your creative juices flowing. I know from experience that some of you will simply take the headlines below and begin using them and you are welcome to do so. However, think for yourself and create a headline that will wow your audience.

1. Your home is worth... (call me I didn't want your mailman to know).

2. Shhhhh.... I've got something I want you to know.(Then on the back...) The value of your Home Home Home

3. I've sold 14 homes this year, make yours number 15.

4. Knock Knock. Who's There? Your Buyer.

5. There is an agent who uses photos of herself over the course of the 25 years she has been in real estate and the headline reads "Although my hairstyles have changed over the years, my service to you has not."

6. Say it with a picture. There is an agent who paints watercolors of each one of her listings and uses that picture as a "just listed" card. This unique idea has captured the attention of the local media who often features her in articles as an agent who is trying something different when marketing a home.

7. Be the first agent to <u>not</u> offer a free property evaluation. This statement is much like a dentist offering to wear rubber gloves during your visit. Property evaluations are what's expected of an agent. Find a stronger

value to offer your readers. Again, this real estate game is about being unique and different. If everyone else is doing it, be the first not to.

Print Advertising
"Early to bed, early to rise—work like hell and advertise."
Peter J. Laurence

Newspaper

Since the Internet has taken shape over the years the newspaper industry has seen a decline in readership and a decline in ad spending. Most of the newspapers in the country are in denial telling their clients that subscriptions have stayed the same and there are just as many people readers today as there were five years ago. Not true. According to stateofthenewsmedia.org, a journalism watchdog of the newspaper industry, the numbers of people who say they read the newspaper regularly have decreased at a rapid rate. When asked if they read a newspaper on a daily basis, only 55% say they do compared to 71% in 1995.

The solution the newspaper companies have missed is that the end result of advertising in the newspaper has changed. No longer are companies looking to sell a product or service as a direct result of a newspaper ad. Instead, companies are using the ads to send the consumer to an area where they are able to look up more information about their product or service; the company website for example.

As an independent agent it is costly and often will not pay off to advertise in a large newspaper. While it may reach a big audience, much of your money is wasted on the thousands of people who are not in the market and not interested in your community. Your money would be better spent in a small community newspaper, which is targeted, cheaper, and relevant to your clients.

Magazines

Like most media, magazines vary greatly in size and cost. The upside is that they are able to reach a very specific audience who are likely to make the time to read each and every page. When personally placing the ads in magazines most real estate agents will wait until they have a listing that would appeal to a group with special interests, which is what magazines are all about. These can include golf communities, communities with their own airstrips, vacation homes, homes with boat access, and more.

The downside of magazine advertising for the independent agent is that not only are they expensive to place, but they also can be expensive to design. Good art direction and messaging become very important in a magazine when standing out among the clutter is crucial to the success of your response.

Direct Marketing

Rick Gasaway, CEO of MarketerNet, a Chicago-based firm that helps businesses target their direct mailings, sums up direct marketing best: "Direct mail is like hunting: You get customers in your cross hairs and take your best shot. Use the right ammunition and you may bag some big game, but only if you precisely identify your quarry."

In 2007, direct mail is expected to reach $64 billion. This is by far the most used medium and in many cases is the absolutely most effective medium to use. It is effective because of the kinds of mailing lists that can be purchased. It is also effective because the United States Post Office has found that 94% of consumers read their mail daily (Deliver Magazine, March, 2005). Need to send a mailing out to men who make more than $3 million a year and own their own airplane? They've got a list. Want to send a mailing out to pet owners that rent an apartment in the city, but make enough to buy a condo that is pet-friendly? There is a list out there. If placing an advertisement on TV is like speaking through a megaphone and hoping that someone hears your message then direct mail is about whispering something very important to someone who is genuinely interested.

You already know the cons of direct mail. As a consumer you know that you receive lots of unsolicited mail. The real question is even if someone looks at a postcard from you for just a few seconds, did that mailing serve a purpose?

Every now and then my wife receives a catalog from Tiffany & Co., the international jeweler. I believe we own two items in our house that are from Tiffany's, which does not make us avid Tiffany customers. However, she still sits down on the couch and thumbs through the small magazine page by page. Shortly afterwards, I caught her talking to her friend about a necklace that she liked in the magazine. To the best of my knowledge her friend owns a few more pieces of Tiffany's then we do. So it begs the question again. Did that magazine serve a purpose even though a purchase hasn't yet been made?

We know that if we send out a postcard to someone, the chances are better that they are not in the market to buy or sell their home. The Mayflower Transit Company found that every year 14% of U.S. citizens move. Eight of these movers are homeowners so when you mail out your materials you can expect only eight people to actually have a need for your services. Doesn't sound promising? Then, look at the bigger picture and you'll see how important regular contact is.

The National Association of Realtors conducted a study in 2006 and found that 70% of consumers forget the name of their Realtor within the first year of buying their home. Additionally, without that regular contact only 35.5% of consumers will use the same agent they used previously. That is not a very large number when you consider these are people you have already worked with. Assuming you served them well, 75% of them should come back to you.

Interestingly enough, most businesses have direct mail wrong. They think direct mail is about standing out in a crowd. Really it is about avoiding crowds altogether.

When planning your direct mail campaign consider the following items:
What lists to purchase
The size of the piece
Paper type
How many pieces
How to word your message
Timing

Total cost
Return on investment

What Lists To Purchase: First decide if you even need to purchase a list. Many real estate companies will offer several ways in which you can obtain qualified leads. However, there are times when you will market specific types of homes that you will need to purchase a list from a vendor like Infousa.com or Equifax.

The Size of the Piece: Determining the size can be difficult. You may only have certain sizes available to you depending on what direct mail service you are using. The most common postcard that is sent out by real estate agents is 4"x6". The next most popular size is 5.5" x 8.5". There haven't been too many scientific studies done to determine which size delivers a better response rate, but there was one multivariable study conducted by Stat-Ease that showed that color in postcard mailings played a larger role in higher response rates than size. Whichever size you choose, practice placing multiple photos on a postcard. As a real estate agent you should have been well educated that the average consumer needs to see at least six photos (preferably more) before they will contact you about a listing. Now that we are in the digital age there is no excuse for not taking many photos of your properties.

How Many Pieces/Timing/Return on Investment? One of the top five questions I get asked when I am on the road refers to how many pieces an agent should send out to get the best response. I call this the magic number. To break it down we have to make certain assumptions. We have to assume that the piece is printed on high quality paper and that the mail is going out to the names and addresses on the sender's blue list. Remember, these are the past clients, friends and family.

Through our friends at Xpressdocs, a direct mail and technology company, we have learned that statistically speaking, if an agent mails 100 postcards per month at 71 cents each they will have spent $852 in a year. If the agent then gets a 1% response rate, which is well under the industry norm, then they will have 12 opportunities a year. Assuming that the agent can close on just 1/3 of these deals, and taking the average home price of $250,000, the gross commission after their 50% split with the company will be $11,250. Not bad, huh? That is a 13,204% return on investment.

However, to achieve these results, mailing cannot be sparse. A minimum of 200 cards each mailing every other month is that magic number to which we are referring. Of course, we are not here to do the minimum, are we?

Paper Type: 50% is how much direct mail pieces can increase their response rates when printed on higher quality paper, according to G.A. Wright Marketing, which found this to be true when it sent identical promotional mailings: one printed with four colors on heavy paper; the other made with three colors on lighter paper. (InMarketing Magazine, Jan. 2006) Clearly paper selection is of the utmost importance to the success of your campaign. You may or may not have direct control of this when designing your piece, but you do have control in choosing a company that uses the best quality paper.

How To Word Your Message: We know that there are three clear methods for your messaging that will improve your response rate.

1. Make it convenient for the consumers. We find that giving the reader a way to look up additional information about you is beneficial. A USPS survey (March, 2005) of direct mail tells us that the majority of consumers will respond to marketing when it is convenient for them. These results remain true in all forms of advertising. Consumers don't always have the time to act right away. By offering a website, the consumer is given a second chance to seek out the product or service when they have time. Also, get out of the habit of withholding the price or address of the home because you think it will force the consumer to call you about the property. They won't. What they will do is look online for the property and discover the information for themselves or find a real estate site that can produce the results they need.

2. Offer something of value. In your messaging, don't forget to offer something of value. Offer a free home cleaning before the listing appointment or a 20% off coupon to a local store that also displays information about you. Make it something unique. "Sending out postcards to consumers with no clear indication on what's in it for them is like throwing your money out the window," says Richard Beck, a direct mail specialist for Marriott Vacations.

3. Quote a past client. We know that 44% of

homeowners will choose their agent based on a referral from a friend or acquaintance. On your materials be sure to include a testimonial so the next time the homeowner hears your name they can say, "I've heard good things about that agent."

4. Use multiple photos and market multiple properties.

If you don't already know it, you should be using six photos or more for every property that you list. If you place yourself in the consumer's shoes, it makes sense that the more you know about a property the more informed your decision will be. Photos provide the reader with more information.

Additionally by marketing multiple properties within the same direct mail piece you are not only extending your advertising budget but letting the reader know that you have a wide range of properties in which you are marketing.

I read a statistic found by Borrell and Associates (2007) that said that only 16% of real estate agents spend their own money on direct mailings. This came as a shock to me because I had always heard that direct mail is where agents spend most of their money. Shortly after reading that I also read that just 20% of the real estate population is making 80% of the income. It goes to show you that there are a lot of real estate professionals out there who believe they can sit back and wait for the clients to come in.

Direct mail is where you should spend the majority of your marketing dollars because it's proven, it's easy—and maybe most importantly—it can be measured.

Direct mail will continue to pave the road to solid leads in real estate. With technology, the direct mail process will graduate into faster printing times, better quality, and more specific targets, which will all but guarantee a better response rate.

Internet Advertising

*"Internet advertising will not replace traditional media,
it will compliment them."*

*"I think that I shall never see
An ad so lovely as a tree.
But if a tree you have to sell,
It takes an ad to do that well."*

~Jef I. Richards, advertising professor from the
University of Texas at Austin

Facts and Figures

According to the Internet Advertising Bureau, in 2008 Internet advertising will surge over $20 billion in total spending. $2 billion of that is spent by the real estate industry. It's hard to believe that just 10 years ago most of us were trying to figure out how the Internet would be useful. Here are the facts as they boil down to the real estate industry from our friends at Borrell and Associates:

61% of agents do not spend any of their own money on Internet advertising.
87% of agents are not buying keywords on Yahoo or Google.
Internet advertising seems to be dominated by new real estate agents. 64% of the less tenured agents were likely to spend money on Internet advertising while only 34% of agents who have 10 years or more in the business were likely to advertise online.

There are a number of ways a real estate professional can use Internet advertising. However, as with any new marketing medium unfamiliar to a real estate agent, it's important firstly to figure out a budget; and secondly, to determine your overall goal in pursuing online advertising. You may simply want to use it as yet another medium in which prospective clients can see you. When determining your goal, ask yourself "what makes my advertisement important to the consumer?" Once you have the answer you have already half-finished your ad.

Forms of Internet Advertising

As a real estate professional there are only a couple of forms of Internet advertising methods to which you should pay attention.

Banner Advertising: Banner ads are a visual approach to placing an advertisement on a specific website. It could be placed on the website of your local newspaper or on a popular real estate website. Banner ads run the spectrum in terms of pricing. Obviously web sites that receive more visits on a daily basis will yield higher ad rates. Using a local newspaper website will often be less expensive and hit a more direct demographic for your business.

Cost Per Click and Search Word Optimization: This is a way in which you can buy key words from a search engine so when a user enters in a subject your ad will pop up among the search engine's choices. Yahoo and Google are the best known search engines that offer this service and costs are very flexible and can be varied around your budget.

Cost per click and search word is where an independent agent's money is best spent. You may be wondering how a search engine even gets to decide what website gets to be the lucky #1. Search engines like Google keep this secret as close to them as possible so others won't take advantage of them, but there are some things we do know. In actuality, your key words are phrases that people will use to conduct their searches. Waterfront homes in Springfield, Big Bear log cabins, starter homes in Anytown—you get the drift. Here are some ideas when buying your key words:

Keywords should be combined with the cities and

regions in which you conduct your business.

Try to give yourself a very specific angle in your market. For example, waterfront homes, 55 and up homes and so on.

List out your words so they are both plural and singular. For example, starter home and starter homes.

Once you discover your keywords, place them on your own website. Use them on your homepage and ask your website to include them in your meta tags. Using the tips above you should be able to edge your way up on the competition.

Whether through banner ads or cost per click ads, Internet advertising can be an appropriate and useful tool in your marketing mix. It's important to remember that it often takes three impressions or more for someone to pick up the phone and hire you as their agent of choice.

Email Marketing is Powerful

We have already discussed the value of direct mail and postcards. Email marketing is of equal importance, but is the area most often ignored by the real estate world. There is so much help these days to take care of the technical side of it so the only thing you need to worry about is the content creation. There are many companies that, for a very small fee, will build your email newsletters for you.

The same rules of advertising apply here as well, but they were never more important simply because it is so easy for a person to hit the delete button. There are some very important factors in email marketing to make sure you and your clients have a mutually beneficial relationship from them.

Send them only to your blue list people and only send them once a quarter. There is no use in bombarding them with information they don't need. These emails are about reminding them that you are out there.

Always give them a chance to opt out of the email subscription. Make sure it is easy for them to do so or you may be on the receiving end of their frustration.

Be brief. If you are going to include an article in your email, display the first few sentences of the article and if they would like to read more have them click a "more" button that will bring them to your website with the remainder of the article. This will also remind them of your webpage.

Show pictures! Always list the past few homes that you have sold. This takes care of the people who don't read and only look at pictures.

Always, always provide all of your contact information in the email.

Outdoor Media
"In advertising, not to be different is virtual suicide"
William Bernbach

Outdoor Media

The first thing a real estate agent will think of when they consider outdoor media or outdoor advertising is billboards. But outdoor media covers much more than mere billboards and when used effectively, it can catapult an agent's name above the rest. It's a broad category and includes shopping cart advertisements; signs in public areas; movie theater advertising; and much more.

Outside the real estate industry, outdoor media has been displayed in areas that were originally ignored. Remember the first time you walked into a rest room only to find advertisements placed near the mirrors or the stalls themselves? Outdoor media is now common in places such as subways, taxi-cab tops, grocery stores, garbage cans, and just about any place you can expect to find a large public gathering. There are over 40 choices in outdoor media. The reality is, that unofficially, outdoor media has been used longer in real estate than any other media. Why? Mostly because the signage that is posted outside a home that's for sale falls within the realm of outdoor media.

Probably the most fascinating part about outdoor advertising is the fact that it is changing just as fast as the Internet. Since it is so broad in scope many are using it as part of their guerilla markcting tactics. For that reason outdoor media can be as large as banners being flown by airplanes to as small as business card placements on grocery carts. The reasons for its successes within the real estate industry is due to the average consumer who are in a hurry and need messaging delivered to them quickly and concisely.

As with anything, determine your goal with outdoor media and then allocate a budget. Do agents generally spend money on outdoor advertising? In 2005 the Outdoor Advertising Association of America reported a $61 million spend from real estate professionals. This excludes the large billboards and monies the corporate real estate offices place. It's not substantial, but when assuming that agents tend to spend money on advertising out of necessity and not industry trends, it opens eyes.

Just like the other forms of advertising, your message will play the most vital role when using outdoor media. It needs to have a clear point and it needs to deliver it quickly.

"Discover what living in Springfield is all about on my blog at MySpringfieldBlog.com." A clear, concise, distinct call to action.

"I sell homes fast. Find out how by emailing me at JaneAgent@springfield.com." A clear, concise, distinct call to action.

Pay Attention To The New Trends
Digital media in the form of outdoor advertising is about to play a big part in your business. Digital signage is popping up everywhere and it is making advertising cheaper and giving you the ability to change your message faster. Taxi-cab tops are the perfect example. There used to be printing costs associated with your ad and a minimum

amount of time that it had to be up. That is no longer the case.

    I've recently spoken to a group in New York City that has asked me to keep them anonymous. What they are doing will not only change the real estate industry, but the way in which we live. Here's what they are doing: Imagine you are living in a luxury condo building. To get into the building you need to scan your access pass to open the lobby doors. This access card will play a large roll in advertising. That access card can pass along information about you to a reader. It can read your name, what building you live in and what company built that building. Let's say that XYZ company built your building. They know you are going to carry that card wherever you go because that is your key to get into your building. XYZ company decides to buy an advertisement in a mall in the form of a television screen with a small RFID reader imbedded in it. The TV will display their logo at all times until someone with an access card walks by it. Once they walk buy the TV a voice comes on and says, "Hello Matt, we know you enjoy living in your condo and would like to tell you about our new condo project that will be completed in 2012."

    To some of you this technology may sound like a Hollywood movie, but I'm here to tell you that this is being tested right now in New York City.
    Realtor.com tells us that real agents tend to spend about 10% of their marketing budgets on outdoor media. When placed correctly 10% of a budget can go a long way.

Public Relations
"The conscious and intelligent manipulation of the organized habits and opinions of the masses is an important element in democratic society."
~Edward Bernays, Father of Public Relations

The Basics of Public Relations

If you are a person who enjoys being in the spotlight and can think fast on your feet, you are going to love the world of public relations. The fact is that very few agents do anything at all to leverage public relations in their business. Good PR is much more than trying to get your name in the paper. The awful part is that these days it's actually very easy to get in the paper, but it is not always for the best reasons. I've heard stories of bad reporters seeking out inexperienced agents just to get them to give a quote that would make a nice negative headline. And it's easy for them to do. Here are some important rules for public relations:

1. When a reporter calls you, ask them if you can call them back in five minutes after you have received approval from your public relations director or your manager. There are a few reasons for this. It's important not to keep a journalist waiting too long because often they have a deadline looming and if kept waiting, they will contact the next agent on their list. Also, calling your PR director or manager covers your butt. Your PR director will want to call the journalist to find out what the story is about and why they chose you to give a quote. This weeds out any chance for a story with bad intentions. If it is a hot button issue or one that may affect the company, the PR director may decide to field the questions herself. She may let you handle the questions, but will want to listen in on the call so she can interject if any red flags go up. This is the only way you should handle a call from a journalist.

2. Nothing is off the record. Just because a reporter shuts the tape recorder off does not mean that the interview is over and you can say whatever you would like. There was a small real estate company in California and the president was being investigated for fraudulent practices. A reporter called an agent, who she knew personally to get the internal scoop. The agent didn't call her manager, but handled herself appropriately during the face-to-face interview. After it was over she finished up by telling her "friend," the reporter, that everyone in the office had suspected for quite some time that the president had been embezzling funds. "He's not that good at his job," she said jokingly, but guess what quote appeared in the paper the next morning? The actual headline of the article was AGENTS SUSPECTED CROWLEY OF FOUL PRACTICES. Everything you say is, in fact, on the record.

3. If it's not interesting, don't try to get it published. So often public relations directors are bombarded with calls from real estate agents who want a press release written because they sold four houses in the same month or they had the biggest year since they started in real estate. That kind of information does not interest the media. If you made the President's Circle for your company, that may be information you can send to your local paper and they may publish it if they have a business section, but do not expect an article written about you. It will probably very simply read: *Jane Realtor of XYZ Company joined the President's Circle for grossing over $50 million in annual sales.*

4. Have your public relations director write your media releases for you. If you do not have a director, ask around to find someone who has written a correct media release. Besides knowing what is newsworthy they have the experience of creating catchy headlines and can format the release appropriately.

Do Good First

The most basic definition of public relations is doing good and telling people about it. Stemming from the days of Rockefeller, public relations has always been about positioning a company or person in the good light of the public eye. The biggest difference between large corporations and you as an individual agent is that the media really doesn't care much about you. Most of the job on the PR side of your business is to get the media to care about what it is you do and what you have accomplished. Often you will have to create your own news, but in doing so, ask yourself one important question. Why would the media, and thus the public, want to know what I am up to? If you do not have an answer to this question then you do not have a newsworthy cause and should not attempt to contact the media about it.

Whether you are approaching a newspaper, magazine or a television show, you need to make sure that you are not wasting their time. Just because you sold more than $5 million in homes last year it does not mean that you are newsworthy. So did 20,000 other agents throughout the country. That may be okay for your small community newspaper... maybe, but certainly not for a regional newspaper.

One person that was great at making her own news for her company was Barbara Corcoran. By producing The Corcoran Report, she gave the media a resource when they needed it. It was informative and it was valuable. It was also great PR for her company.

You may find that by introducing yourself to local reporters and asking them if they would like to receive information from time to time about current real estate trends they will agree and more often than not call you for a quote. A reporter will not write about the real estate market every single article, but when they do and you have opened up the door of communications, you will be the first person they think of when they need something from and estate agent.

Interview With a Real Estate Reporter
One of the best ways to figure out how to be heard is to go directly to the person who is doing all of the talking. I decided to sit down with a reporter from the Boston Globe who asked me to keep her name anonymous and ask a few questions that may help us with the best methods in contacting reporters.

How many real estate-related press releases do you receive a day?
Between 5 and 10.

How many of these are truly newsworthy?
Almost none. The only newsworthy press releases I receive are the monthly sales and price reports from two sources.

How do you find a real estate agent to interview for a story?
I interview some that I've interviewed in the past or if I want to know about what's happening in a specific town, I'll do a Google search for an agent. I try to call agents from a variety of companies.

What are your pet peeves when it comes to real estate companies and agents?
Some agents do not talk about how the market really is. They talk about how they want it to be.

What kind of stories are you looking for?
Unique things that happen with respect to a specific property, a market, solid trend stories, fraudulent activities, unfair practices, news. Stories about what buyers and sellers are doing differently.

Which way do you prefer that an agent contact you?
Email is easier. I can't answer every call.

What kind of information do you find yourself looking for most often?
I'm constantly trying to find agents who will help me by asking a client—either a buyer or seller—to talk to me. That's the toughest part—especially buyers.

Reporters are inundated with unnecessary calls from real estate agents with story ideas that really aren't stories at all. You'll also notice that reporters are looking for very unique stories—something that is different to what the public is used to hearing about. One thing I like to do before I call a reporter for any paper is try to predict a headline for the story that I am trying to pitch. If I know I can't create a clever headline that sounds interesting, chances are it may not be the most newsworthy story. What story would you rather read? "Judy Salesperson Sells Her Third One Million Dollar Home" or "Luxury Market Takes Off Despite Slowing Market." The real trick is that you need to present a story that affects as many people as possible.

Just as Barbara Corcoran found a way to become a resource to the media by producing The Corcoran Report, so can you. You have regular access to these reports. Reporters need to quote statistics from real estate companies to give their story credibility. It's just one way you can open up the doors of communication between you and the media.

What Can You Do To Get Publicity?
There are some ways in which to receive publicity based on your activities, but they don't happen overnight. It takes a lot of hard work and time to be noticed. Some of the things you can do to receive publicity are:
Become a speaker
Write an article
Offer to be quoted in an article
Become a resource

Appear on a radio/talk show
Be accessible/easy to reach
Host a community event

All of these will take some serious effort on your part, but the payoff is big. It's difficult to place a price tag on good publicity.

Online Social Networks

Online social networks include names that you have heard before, but may not understand why they are so widely used. These names include My Space, Facebook, and LinkedIn. All three of these sites are better known as social networking sites.

Although they won't result in direct leads very often, making these social networks are an important part of your marketing mix. Each one takes only a short time to build, but before you know it, you have 100 friends with whom you can communicate directly. The days are long gone when these social networking tools were just for teeny-boppers.

Facebook has become one of my favorite sites, mainly because of its ability to use RSS feeds. RSS makes it possible for people to keep up with their favorite web sites in an automated manner that's easier than checking them manually. The technology seems to be far above the rest. It is very easy to add applications and special feeds from other sites that you may be interested in.

One of the best parts of creating your social online

community is that very easily you will exponentially increase the number of people that read your blog. This, in turn, will get your personal website to climb the search engine ladder to the top of many searches.

Don't forget about professional sites that you can turn to, like Active Rain. Active Rain is a twist on MySpace, Facebook, and LinkedIn. It was designed specifically for real estate agents to assist with referrals and is a wealth of information with its blogs from real estate agents and professionals all over the United States.

Blogging

A blog or a web log is a website where entries are written on just about any subject you can think about. Some blogs are sparse in their subject matter like personal journals, and other blogs can be directed at a specific hobby or industry, such as real estate. A company called Technorati is said to have tracked over 71 million blogs as at May 2007.

Since blogs have begun, they have opened up a dialogue between the author who begins the discussion and anyone who reads it. Surprisingly, few real estate agents believe blogging is a practice relevant to them. I disagree. Adding your professional opinion of the local market conditions and trends is invaluable to your community and can really give your personal website added value. The great news is that since blogging is not new in the world, there are many sites that will host your blogs and you will be able to direct traffic from your own personal website to these sites.

A Boston Globe article written in April, 2007 talked about Keith, a local Boston real estate agent, who began his blog as a way to get feedback from his clients. "I thought that it would be a good way to create communications between buyers, sellers and me," he said. Within months, Keith noticed that his business was picking up. He was getting leads from a younger audience and from house hunters located outside the Boston metro area—consumers who needed the Internet to search for their home. Additionally, it placed his website in the top of Google's searches for Boston real estate. Like most real estate blogs out there Keith's site did something very important. It created a large amount of local information and positioned itself as a valuable local real estate source.

If you remember back to the chapter on websites you will recall the importance of adding a blog on your website. It gives you a very distinctive tool that no one else can offer or copy. Remember these are your thoughts and opinions, and as a professional in the real estate industry this is vital to your business.

It should also be stated that blogging is very contagious in the sense that it spreads through social mediums just like MySpace and Facebook. Blogs will often reference other blogs that people have found to be interesting. When you write important information other people will link directly to your blog giving you visibility for your efforts.

Maybe one of the best things agents have going

for them is that blogging is still very new to all industries and since historically the real estate industry lags behind in technology there is still a lot of time to position yourself as a blogging pioneer.

Just some of the sites out there to help you get started include blogger.com, typepad.com, squarespace.com, mytypes.com, and probably a thousand others. These sites take all of the technical know-how of creating a blog and give you only one thing to do. Type.

Before you can begin your own blog you need to find out what's already out there. How are they set up? Can readers respond easily? The following are sites to help you out as you create your blog.

Freshome.com: This site is not specific to real estate, but covers areas such as staging a home, new gadgets for homes, new trends in vacation homes, and much more.

BiggerPockets.com: You will notice a section specifically on this site called real estate blog. This blog has a national reach and still covers important topics that every real estate professional encounters.

TheRealEstateBloggers.com: The title says it all. You will notice a large following of New York City agents on the site, which leads me to believe is that this is where the site found its beginning. It's one of the more dedicated sites to real estate you will find on the Internet.

BlogofGeese.com: A shameless plug for my own blog read by many agents throughout the U.S. If you like what you are reading now, it only gets better.

Active Rain: If you haven't seen this yet, you are missing a big one! Maybe it should be at the top of this list. Think of it as a MySpace for real estate agents, but this one has content you can actually use for your business. Great tips from agents all throughout the US!

Take a look at each one of these sites and find out why so many real estate professionals read them on a daily basis. Once you look at the above links start visiting some of your favorite companies to find out if they have a blog that you may have missed before. They serve as valuable tools for your business.

Go Guerilla
"Guerrilla marketing says you don't need to spend money if you're willing to invest time, energy, imagination, and knowledge."
Jay Conrad Levinson,
Godfather of Guerilla Marketing

Huh?

My first experience with guerilla advertising was when I went to the Boston Marathon back in 2005. My wife and I were enjoying the first beautiful spring day of the year. There was a distraction though. Many people were walking by me and they had something stamped to their forehead. I didn't notice what it said on the first person that walked by me. The second one I saw clearly, although I was trying not to stare because who knows what kind of wacko this was. After all he was wearing a stamp on his forehead! It read: Terry Tate. Of course I now noticed that all of the people with the stamps on their forehead were also wearing the same shirt.

Reebok was using a guerilla tactic to spread the word of a new campaign that used a fictitious football linebacker named Terry Tate. Some of you may remember the commercial. Terry was the office linebacker that would tackle anyone who wasn't really working. For me, this is what began my fascination with guerilla marketing.

The truth is that no one really wants to reveal the true definition of guerilla marketing. They want it to sound mysterious and confusing, so large companies have to hire a firm or the "experts" to conduct their guerilla marketing. I'm going to spoil the mystery. Guerilla marketing is a formal organization of instigating word-of-mouth about your product or service. The reason the real estate industry will embrace this in the years to come is that it is unconventional marketing intended to get maximum results using minimal resources. I'm not saying that real estate agents are cheap; I'm saying they're frugal.

In the case of Terry Tate, it got people talking around the Boston Metro. Who is Terry Tate? Why did they have that on their forehead? Finally it bothered me so much that I needed to look up the website that was displayed on their T-shirts to find out what it was all about. It got me to their site, but I still haven't owned a pair of Reeboks since I was in 8th grade. Does that make the campaign ineffective? No, I don't think so. After all I'm telling all of you about it.

The Value of Word of Mouth
So much of the success of guerilla marketing is owed to word of mouth advertising. In fact you can call guerilla marketing an instigator or the flint of word of mouth advertising. Using it can result in an organic growth of your business that will hit you like a slap in the face on a cold day. Some of you will ask, "Why do we have to focus on word of mouth if it grows organically?" The answer is simple. It only grows once you plant the seed and that is where guerilla marketing comes back into play. Guerilla marketing is the "how to" of planting the seed. Dr. Pilotta, Professor of Communications at Ohio State University, once said, "...marketers can no longer operate on the assumption that viewers are actually giving their message undivided attention... the biggest consumer buying influencer of all is word of mouth."

In recent years guerilla marketing has received more and more attention, though not always positive. In

2007, a small guerilla marketing company called Interference, placed small light boxes around the city of Boston to promote a cartoon called Aqua Teen Hunger Force. The stunt ended up making the national spotlight as citizens of Boston thought the light boxes were planted by terrorists. The ordeal sent a whirlwind of talk in the guerilla marketing about negative publicity and if it is really negative or not.

The subject of this new wave of marketing is so new it won't be talked about in the real estate world for years to come. This is mainly because many of its tactics have not yet been tested or even thought of for that matter. However, it doesn't make the subject any less important for you to consider. In fact, now is the time to begin thinking about how guerilla marketing applies to your business and what you can do to pioneer it in your area.

Guerilla Tactics

Keep in mind that guerilla marketing is so much about the consumer "discovering" the information that you have planted for them and having them believe that it was never planted in the first place. Think about musicians. So many people out there want to discover the next best musician that they will refer their friends in an almost secret fashion. "Hey there is this new band and they aren't well known yet, but you need to check them out before they get big."

This is often how books are sold. "Have you heard about Jane Author? She is a phenomenal writer." Books are a strange thing because when someone recommends a book to me, I feel obligated to check it out so I am able to report back to them about what I thought about the book.

In both of these examples, the word of mouth began and created a secret society of sorts. People felt like they were in on something good that not many knew about.

Real Estate agents can fall in this same category and already do. "I have used the same agent for years; you need to use her. You'll love her." This is how the majority of agents will receive their business.

The question then becomes, "How does one instigate this conversation? Is there a way to manufacture word of mouth?" This is where guerilla marketing comes in. Here are some of the latest and greatest ways to create buzz about you!

1. All great things come in a package. Create a plain black box tied with ribbon. Place in it your business card, a small card of information about you and your business, a small engraved gift of some sort. You should have about 10 of these things on standby at all times. Any time you hear anyone in town thinking of selling their home, give them this gift. It's better if you can find an acquaintance of theirs who already knows you and have them give the package for you.

2. Offer to print out yard sale signs for anyone who may be holding one at their home. At the bottom of

every sign will be an advertisement for your business.

3. Show off your listings with a digital photo frame. Walk into a dentist's office, a doctor's office, or a restaurant and ask them if you can place a digital photo frame on an eye-level shelf to display your listings. These photo frames can be found at every major store, such as Target, Sears, and Wal-Mart. The only other thing you need is a memory card and an easy to use program that will allow you to write prices over your listing. Make sure that in between every three listings your business card pops up.

4. Offer a cleaning service as part of your overall package. Three hours of cleaning free. What a great stress reliever for your homeowners to know they won't have to clean their place before their first open house.

5. Have something outrageous as your slogan and send a press release about it to your local papers. "If I don't sell your home within 90 days, I'll work for you for free."

6. For $80 a month, the Property Source Network will allow you to offer a $50,000 sweepstakes quarterly drawing entry to any of your homeowners. This gives you an added edge on your competition without having to pay out $50,000 of your own money.

As an inexpensive way to get your word out, guerilla marketing takes high involvement and constant innovation. Keep your eyes on sites like gmarketing.com to develop new ideas around your business.

Wrap-Up
"I've seen a lot of things come to an end, but where is this fat lady everyone talks about?"
~Matthew Gosselin

It Has Been Fun!

Successful real estate is about taking the right action to catapult your name over the others in your area. Very few agents will take the time to develop their business and to ask themselves, "What makes me so special?" By reading this book you are already one step ahead of those people. However, observing what is supposed to be done and actually committing yourself to take action are two different ballgames.

Your career in real estate should be one in which continued education is required. The technology changes quickly. Use it to your benefit. The laws change frequently, keeping you on your toes. But the most important aspect of real estate remains at the grassroots level. It is about serving others and building relationships. You have an uphill battle because consumers in general have very high expectations. They want the best and they want it yesterday. They want to believe that there is no one else in the world that you want to please more than them. And you need to try to make them believe that.

I'll leave you with some great words from Seth Godin, the self-acclaimed marketing guru.

"It seems to me that insulation from discontent comes from building a relationship. From real people. Relationships that make us feel counted upon, respected, trusted and valued cut through the ennui of dissatisfaction. We got ourselves into this mess by acting like smart marketers, and as marketers we can get out of it by acting like people."

Good skill to you and your business. I will see you on the road!

Stay up to date with My Blue Goose by visiting www.MyBlueGoose.com
or view the blog at
www.BlogofGeese.com.

Credits

There are so many people to thank for their efforts, inspiration, knowledge, and involvement in putting My Blue Goose together. At the top of the list is my wife—for putting up with my endless babble every night about real estate subjects that aren't really included in her list of hobbies. I'm guessing this will continue. Thank you to the entire team at Xpressdocs, a company whose integrity and commitment is contagious. Thank you to all of those who have inspired me to write this book and whether they knew it or not, played a role in the creation of the book: Barbara Corcoran, Seth Godin, Hugh MacLeod, Michele Giordano and team, Melissa and Holly over at PFR, Phyllis Pezenik, Dan Corthell, Scott Hurley, Amy Crouch, Colin Baily, Brian Naughton, Eric Arnold, Laurel Strand. Thank you to Karen Block-Nichols for the design hours she committed to the project.

Lastly, thank you to all of the real estate professionals I have met over the years who have helped me to understand their 'take' on the real estate world.

Index

A
Advertising 6-7, 31-32, 71-73, 76-77, 81-83, 88-89, 91-94, 97-100, 114-115
Agents 6, 15-17, 19-20, 23-27, 29-31, 35, 37, 44-48, 50, 54-57, 61, 64-67, 72, 83, 86, 89, 92, 99-100, 102-104, 106-107, 109-112, 115, 117, 122
Authentic 6, 16

B
Basics 6-7, 21, 29-30, 37, 75, 102
Blogging 7, 109-111
Blue Goose 1, 4, 6, 11, 13-16, 19-20, 61, 67, 71, 124
Blue List 6, 42-44, 48-51, 87, 95

C
Company 6, 10, 17, 22, 25-27, 29-31, 33, 36, 38, 42-45, 49, 54-56, 58-59, 63-65, 67-68, 82, 85, 87, 100, 102-105, 109, 116, 124
Consumers 6, 17, 38, 43, 63, 67, 84-85, 88, 110, 122
Contacts 6, 43-45
Corcoran, Barbara 13, 105, 107, 124

D
Direct Mail 7, 24, 31, 61, 83-90, 94

E
Email 7, 19, 48, 55, 59, 63, 72, 94-95, 106

G
goose 1, 4, 6, 11, 13-16, 19-20, 61, 67, 71, 124
Guerilla 7, 48-49, 98, 113-117, 119

I
Internet 6-7, 27, 31, 39, 53, 56-59, 82, 91-94, 98, 110-111

J
Journalist 7, 102

M
Magazines 7, 76, 83
Market 16-17, 25, 27-28, 33-34, 38, 43-45, 47, 51, 61, 66, 82, 85-86, 89, 94, 105-107, 109
marketing 1, 4, 6-7, 10-11, 16-20, 23, 28-30, 32-33, 36, 47-49, 60, 62, 65, 78, 83, 87-90, 92, 94-95, 98, 100, 108, 113-117, 119, 122, 125
Media 7, 17, 64, 78, 83, 91, 97-100, 103-105, 107

N
Newspaper 7, 74, 82, 93, 104

O
Outdoor 7, 97-100

P
Public Relations 7, 17, 101-104
publicity 7, 107-108, 116

R
real estate 1, 4, 6, 10-11, 15-17, 19, 22-27, 29-32, 34-35, 37-38, 42-48, 50, 54-55, 57-68, 77-79, 83, 86, 88-90, 92-94, 98-100, 103, 105-107, 109-112, 114-117, 122, 124-125

S
Social Networks 7, 108

T
Technology 6, 16, 22, 25, 47, 53-56, 58, 62-67, 87, 90, 100, 108, 111, 122

W
Web Page 6, 61
Websites 6, 58-60, 65, 68, 110
Word of Mouth 7, 32, 115, 117